WIN
AT WORK

WIN AT WORK

DAILY DEVOTIONS FOR YOUR WORK WEEK THAT WILL **TRANSFORM** HOW YOU LIVE AND LEAD

MARK C. OVERTON

Win at Work

Copyright © 2023 by Mark C. Overton. All rights reserved.

No part of this publication may be reproduced, stored in a retrieval system, or transmitted by any means, electronic, mechanical, photocopy, recording, or otherwise, without the author's prior permission except as provided by USA copyright law.

The opinions expressed by the author are not necessarily those of URLink Print and Media.

1603 Capitol Ave., Suite 310 Cheyenne, Wyoming USA 82001
1-888-980-6523 | admin@urlinkpublishing.com

URLink Print and Media is committed to excellence in the publishing industry.

Book design copyright © 2023 by URLink Print and Media. All rights reserved.

Published in the United States of America

Library of Congress Control Number: 2023916682
ISBN 978-1-68486-617-5 (Paperback)
ISBN 978-1-68486-513-0 (Digital)

07.08.23

Contents

WorkWeek # 1   Demonstrating GODLY CHARACTER 13
Day 1   Integrity 15
Day 2   Service 17
Day 3   Excellence 19
Day 4   Courage 21
Day 5   Loyalty 23

WorkWeek # 2   WORKING HEARTILY 25
Day 1   Ability 27
Day 2   Success 29
Day 3   Promotion 31
Day 4   Diligence 34
Day 5   Balance 36

**WorkWeek # 3   MODELING ATTRIBUTES OF
                 GODLY EMPLOYEES 39**
Day 1   Prayerfulness 41
Day 2   Obedience 43
Day 3   Attitude 44
Day 4   Encouragement 46
Day 5   Faithfulness 48

WorkWeek # 4   LEADING AND BEYOND 51
Day 1   Direction 53
Day 2   Communication 55
Day 3   Ambition 57
Day 4   Team 59
Day 5   Transitioning 61

Preface

THE AVERAGE PERSON WILL SPEND approximately 150,000 hours at work in their lifetime, which implies that they spend about 40 percent of their waking life at work. And many people believe that God and laboring don't mix: the competitive, cutthroat demands of the working world versus the compassion and love of Christians. Yet right from the start of the Bible, God was at work in creation, finishing the work he had been doing and resting on the seventh day.

Work is so important. He says you shall work six days. Work (and rest) are ways in which you imitate him.

Scripture mentions the words *work* and *toil* over 480 times in the Bible, supporting the importance of work to God. The Apostle Paul, who modeled working night and day laboring and toiling, also underlines the significance of work: If you're not willing (rather than people who are not physically or mentally unable to work) to work, you're not ready to eat either.

Regardless of your profession, diversity, and inclusion in the workplace, working from home, the office, or a hybrid working model, work often needs more satisfaction. Your typical workweek behavior may spiral from the Monday Morning Blues to Hump Day Wednesday to Living for Friday. Have you reached a breaking point where you desire to say, "I'm out of here!" Should you stay, or should you go?

During the COVID-19 pandemic, many American workers quit their jobs while U.S. employers had more positions to fill than ever before. People leave bad jobs because of bad bosses or poor management who don't appreciate their value.

Today job seekers are shopping for the best opportunity (e.g., work passion, new opportunities aligning better with your interests and values, chances to move up, flexibility in working hours and location, etc.). But, of course, you can care for others and look out for your needs too. If that's you, become an insider with *Win at Work*, and you can suddenly find more excellent and proven satisfaction in your job and also be an ambassador for Christ.

Jesus called you to go out to all the world and make disciples of all nations. God blesses you to be a blessing to the whole world.

Today you may only have to travel a little, depending on where you live. In some metropolitan cities, the area represents practically every nation.

You are his representative on earth. Through you, he appeals for you to reconcile others to him. You request them to become his follower and ambassadors themselves.

Love is the motive, message, and means! So this responsibility and urgent work of telling everyone the Good News is huge.

Unfortunately, the worst and only picture of Christ some people will see is you. Therefore, it is essential that you immediately develop and improve your powerful platform as a remarkable witness in shining armor at your work for the glory of his kingdom, God's nation.

Do everything you say or do in the name of the Lord Jesus.

Always give thanks to God the Father through Christ (Col. 3:17). Pursuing excellence is nothing more than mirroring his character and behavior. It's easier when you are excited about your job to instantly turn the focus of your work from "I'm doing this for my boss" or "I'm doing this to get paid" to "I'm doing this for the lord."

Accordingly, start your day with God first, giving thanks, reading, or listening to praise music. Then, I encourage you to focus on him from when you get up until you leave for work. But, no, it doesn't end there. Continuous worship is another book.

As a *fellow worker*, this devotional will fully equip you to increase your role as an ambassador, especially since you spend most of your life in the workplace.

It helps teach us what is true. It helps correct our mistakes. It helps make our lives whole again. It helps train us to do what is right (2 Tim. 3:16–17).

Whatever work God calls you to do will probably occupy much of your life. It's part of what he created you to do and will also be part of what you do in heaven.

Like Priscilla and Aquila, coworkers in Christ, and the value of Paul's work, your work also has lasting value. Your hard work will outlive you.

Your work's ultimate value reflects that God, too, is a worker. Therefore, like Mary, who worked very hard for him, give yourself entirely to his work—the work of the Gospel.

Like opening an email from a secure source, you can trust the sender without risk. However, this hot message isn't from an anonymous informant; it's from God, who has given you a big job.

As one of the few, your job as his ambassador to the people around you is distinguished. But first, you need to understand the job description before you can do a job well.

According to Wikipedia, "an ambassador is the highest-ranking diplomat representing a nation." Ambassadors are skilled at representing their country by both how they act and what they say. They're ministers of the highest rank sent to a foreign court to represent the country's sovereignty (e.g., a British ambassador denotes the queen and country wherever the authority sends them). Thus, recognizing who you are as Christ's ambassador is an immense privilege!

You might ask, "How do I expertly promote his exclusive kingdom?" First, completely walk in the fruit of the Spirit. But the fruit the Holy Spirit produces is love, joy, and peace. It is being patient, kind, and generous. It is being faithful and gentle and having control of oneself. There is no law against things of that kind (Gal. 5:22–23).

God wants you to accurately represent him to the world, including those outside his kingdom. So he supplies you with the fantastic message he wants you to take to the world. He brings us back to Himself through Christ's death on the cross and has given us the task of getting others back to him through Christ.

He has trusted us with the message that people may be returned to him (2 Cor. 5:18–19).

Through you, God is urging all people to suddenly become reunited with him through the work of his son, Jesus Christ. And for this reason, you can instantly rise and shine as an ambassador, accepting an extraordinary privilege on behalf of him those around you. Work is one area where you can boost his message by buckling down and being your best.

> Slaves [workers], obey your earthly masters in everything. Don't do it to please them when they are watching you. Obey them with an honest heart. Do it out of respect for the Lord. Work at everything you do with all your heart. Work as if you were working for the Lord, not for human masters. Work because you know you will finally receive what the Lord wants you to have as a reward. You are slaves of the Lord Christ.
> (Col. 3:22–24)

By opening this book, you've shown interest in where you are and your desire to be. In this inspiring devotional, you'll find its content structured into four five-day workweek-based sections. Discover how each unit inspires you to get what you want from your job and be an excellent ambassador.

- Workweek # 1 encompasses "Demonstrating Godly Character."
- Workweek # 2 reveals our part in "Working Heartily."
- Workweek # 3 encourages "Modeling Attributes of Godly Employees."
- Finally, Workweek # 4 examines "Leading and Beyond."

In your capacity as an ambassador, *Win at Work* can accelerate making a kingdom impact now by meeting your pressing need to be the best you can be at your job. You can anticipate this encouraging devotional, faithfully representing and advancing his reconciliation message.

- Do you want to be thoroughly equipped for every good work?
- Do you desire to be rewarded for your hard work?
- God gives you your abilities and controls success and promotion. How should this perspective affect your work?
- For whom do you work in truth? How will this understanding change your work performance?
- What steps will you take to earn more job satisfaction, leadership skills, responsibilities and respect, and significance and say about how you do things, as well as privileges, pay, and prestige?
- In leadership, you gain more positions (you can become more), power and influence (you can do more), and privilege (you can have more). *Win at work* can apply this to your situation now.

Act now and apply this book at work; it delivers solutions for your work goals directly, instantly fulfilling your job satisfaction needs materially and spiritually.

Work! Work! Work! You can make an impact now by becoming a *giant* ambassador for the *home kingdom* of God and a *champ* for him in your work rather than a *chump* for men.

The honor and reputation of the kingdom are in your hands, and today is your new life of suddenly achieving victory and job satisfaction—with him, all things are possible.

Work your way to a successful you. Hard work pays off. Do your best to please God and win at work.

WorkWeek # 1

Demonstrating GODLY CHARACTER

Day 1

Integrity

> Suppose a man makes a unique promise to the Lord. Or suppose he gives his Word to do something. Then he must keep his promise. He must do everything he said he would do.
>
> —Num. 30:2

YOU MAY HAVE WATCHED THE drama unfolding from the "Honesty Pass It On" commercial. A teenager runs across town with a purse a woman forgot at a bus stop. You may wonder if the young man is stealing or returning the bag until the last triumphant moment. He instantly returns the purse, and on-duty police officers reward him with a doughnut. We need more people doing the right thing and valuing integrity.

As a supervisor, I remember correcting workers who cooked the books or pencil whipped a safety or compliance inspection checklist or training record. You may find it reassuring when your workers own their mistakes by immediately taking responsibility for having made them or admitting to something when no one knew they did it.

Daniel 6:4 also shows that "*the* two leaders and the royal rulers looked for a reason to bring charges against Daniel. They tried to find something wrong with how he ran the government, but they couldn't. They couldn't find any fault with his work. They could always trust him. He never did anything wrong and always did what he was supposed to." His *haters* could find no dishonesty in him, and there was no "evidence of corruption" in his work. The king trusted him.

Integrity is the basis of trust. Trust makes leaders effective; integrity underpins belief, which involves character and competence. Therefore, one of the primary purposes of work is character development. When you build your *house* at work, the *house* is also making you (e.g., your ability, knowledge, judgment, and so forth).

People who excel keep their Word; they are reliable. So you count on them to do what they say they'll do.

> *Father, thank you for your Word, a lamp to my feet and light for my path. To live is Christ and help me to do the right thing. May my integrity characterize me as it honors you, my heavenly Father? In Jesus's name, I pray, amen.*

Day 2

Service

> None of you should look out just for your good. However, each of you should also look out for the good of others.
>
> —Phil. 2:4

WHILE I SERVED IN THE United States Air Force, the oath of enlistment's language makes followership-leadership a necessity of service:

> And I will obey the orders of the President of the United States. The charges of the officers appointed over me, according to regulations and the Uniform Code of Military Justice. Service is a pathway to real significance. Significance isn't possible unless what we do suddenly contribute to the welfare of others. Dr. Martin Luther King Jr. once said, "Life's most persistent and urgent question is: 'What are you doing for others?'"

In John 13:12–15, Jesus also modeled an example of servant leadership to his disciples. When (he) finished washing their feet, he put on his clothes and returned to his place.

> "Do you understand what I have done for you?" he asked them. "You call me 'Teacher' and 'Lord.' You are right. That is what I am. I, your Lord and Teacher, have washed your feet. It would help if you also washed one another's feet. I have given you an example. It would be best if you did as I have done for you.

The night before the authority ordered Jesus' crucifixion, he washed his disciples' feet.

The Lord performed what may be considered a common task. Likewise, when you shift your focus from serving your own needs and desires to operating from the heart the needs of others first, you truly experience your passion and give your best for him. Absolute joy comes from serving Jesus, others, and yourself last (JOY).

> *Heavenly Father, allow me to humbly serve others with a joyful heart, always giving and never expecting to receive. Let me help others as you do, sharing my talents, time, and energy. Thank you, Lord; I give you all the glory, honor, and praise. In Jesus's name, amen.*

Day 3

Excellence

> Daniel did a better job than the other two leaders, or even any of the royal rulers, for that matter. He was an unusually good and able man. So the king planned to put him in charge of the whole kingdom.
> —Dan. 6:3

ONE ROLE OF A COMPUTER technician is to perform initial fault assessment and resolution in response to customer-reported incidents via trouble tickets.

While working as a computer technician, assigned computer incidents frequently remained unresolved in the job tracking system. As a result, technicians often kept many incidents in their job queue without taking appropriate, timely action to resolve them. As a result, managers may have perceived that workers did the minimum instead of resolving current incidents to delay the assignment of new incidents.

In illustrating excellence, the story of the "camel test" is a familiar one. Abraham's servant would ask a young maiden for a sip of water, and if she offered to provide water for his camels as well, she would be the one—a suitable wife for Abraham's son, Isaac.

Genesis 24:17–20 tells us that:

> The servant hurried to meet her. He said, "Please give me a little water from your jar." "Have a drink, sir," she said. She quickly lowered the jar to her hands and gave him a drink. After she had given him a drink, she said, "I'll get water for your camels too. I'll keep doing it until they have had enough to drink."

So she quickly emptied her jar into the stone tub. Then she ran back to the well to get more water. Finally, she got enough for all the servant's camels.

Rebecca became Isaac's bride!
Booker T. Washington once said, "Excellence is to do a common thing in an uncommon way."
Some say Rebecca may have drawn water for ten thirsty camels. However, camels can drink up to forty gallons in one session. Thus, Rebecca drew as much as four hundred gallons of water!
You can also raise *your game* and give God your best. You can exceed what others expect of you. Do more than the minimum; don't just get by. You can receive more than you wish and rise to the top. Suppose someone forces you to go one mile. Go two miles with them (Matt. 5:41).

> *Father, you are the Most High. I use the gifts given to me and let my light shine before men so they may see my excellence and praiseworthy deeds. To God be all glory, honor, and praise. Amen.*

Day 4

Courage

Be on your guard. Remain firm in the faith. Be brave.
—1 Cor. 16:13

WHILE THE US AIR FORCE DEPLOYED ME TO Qatar, my commander and I visited Iraq to look at forward operating bases' airmen's welfare and mission contributions. Before departing, a friend dropped me a note meant to reflect God's protection. While confident in him as my *rock*, sun, and shield from harm's way, the message was uplifting and thoughtful. It echoed divine faith and courage in him always.

We're also reminded in Hebrews 11:23–24, 27 that courage always produces action.

> Moses' parents had faith. So they hid him for three months after he was born. They saw that he was a unique child, and they were not afraid of the king's command. Moses had faith, so he refused to be called the son of Pharaoh's daughter. That happened after he had grown up. Because of his faith, Moses left Egypt. It wasn't because he was afraid of the king's anger. Moses didn't let anything stop him. That's because he saw God people can't see. He persevered because he saw him who was invisible.

Upholding standards of conduct and personal ethics as a centerpiece in your life and work also demands great courage. Minimum standards are needed. Strive to avoid even the perception of abusing your position, misusing time or funds, stealing, hazing, being deceitful, or taking part in any other unprofessional or prohibited actions.

Step away from battles or giants that would hold you back from your goals, trying to be like others; trying to make everybody happy; too many hobbies or too much time spent on a hobby; nonstop browsing or viewing of social media, movies, or television— the wrong kinds of relationships; past mistakes, and so on. Instead, build up your faith and keep your foot from their path.

> *Eternal Father, I am of good courage and pray you to grant me with all boldness to speak forth your Word. I believe no weapon formed against me shall prosper. I trust in you wholeheartedly and lean not to my understanding. In all my ways, I acknowledge you, and you direct my path, and I walk in the light of your Word. In Jesus's name, amen.*

Day 5

Loyalty

Commit to the Lord in everything you do. Then he will make your plans succeed.

—Prov. 16:3 (N.I.R.V.)

MOST PEOPLE RECITE WEDDING VOWS pledging commitment and loyalty to their new spouse till "death us do part." So naturally, we all crave such unwavering devotion in our marriages.

In my marriage, my better half and I covenant and honor *"MO2-4L+"—Mark and Margarita Overton for Life Joyfully.* Commitment and loyalty are also reflected in faithful allegiances between lifelong friends, college graduates, and their alma mater, between veterans and the armed services, and even between citizens and their countries.

In 1 Samuel 20:13–16, we see Jonathan and David's remarkable friendship and loyalty.

> But suppose he wants to harm you. And I don't let you know about it. Suppose I don't help you get away in peace. Then may the Lord punish me greatly. May he be with you, just as he has been with my Father? But, of course, always be kind to me, just as the Lord is. Be kind to me as long as I live. Then folk won't kill him. And never stop being kind to my family. Don't stop even when the Lord has cut off every one of your enemies from the face of the earth." So Jonathan made a covenant of friendship with David and his family.
>
> He said, "May the Lord hold David's enemies responsible for what they've done."

Similarly, as an employee, honor your employer sincerely by rendering service with goodwill as you do to the Lord. Likewise, make your chief commitment to God himself.

> The Lord looks out over the whole earth. He gives strength to those who commit their lives entirely to him. You have done a foolish thing. From now on, you will be at war.
>
> (2 Chron. 16:9)

Awesome Father, in the name of Jesus, I commit my way to you. You will cause my thoughts to become agreeable to your will, and so shall my plans be established and succeed. I praise You and promise to live according to Your Word. Amen.

WorkWeek # 2

WORKING HEARTILY

Day 1

Ability

> Every skilled worker to whom the Lord has given skill and ability. They know how to do all the work for every purpose connected with the sacred tent. And that includes setting it up.
>
> —Exod. 36:1

WHEN I LED PROJECTS AT work, I frequently heard, "20 percent of the people are doing 80 percent of the work," which follows the Pareto principle or the 80/20 rule.

In 1906, an economist observed that 20 percent of the people in Italy owned 80 percent of the land. This same principle that 20 percent of something is always responsible for 80 percent of the results can apply in various work situations.

First Corinthians 12:27 tells us, "You are the body of Christ. Each one of you is a part of it."

God has given each of us a specific calling or purpose. Ephesians 2:10 (NIRV) underscores, "We are God's creation. He created us to belong to Christ Jesus. Now we can do good work. Long ago, God prepared these works for us to do." Exodus 36:1 also illustrates this truth in the above scripture.

God has given you unique aptitudes. He provides job skills. You are gifted uniquely—spiritual gifts, heart, abilities, personality, and experiences.

David was a shepherd and a king. Luke was a doctor. Lydia was a retailer of purple fabric. Daniel was a government worker. Paul was a tentmaker. Mary was a homemaker. Jesus was a carpenter.

Each of us has a role, and every part is just as important. Some are visible, some are behind the scenes, but all are valuable. You are given gifts for a reason. You *are* responsible for the ones given to you.

Develop your talents. Keep learning, growing, and improving; sharpen your skills. Be a good steward of your gifts, not for selfish uses but for the good of others. When you use your gifts to serve others, you help equip everybody to do something versus only the 20 percent. Rise and give; rise and build.

> *Father, I thank you for filling me with talents and skills and the knowledge of your will to be concerned for not only my interests but also the interest of others. I give you all the praise, honor, and glory. In Jesus's name, amen.*

Day 2

Success

> May he give you what your heart wishes for?
> May he make all your plans succeed?
> —Ps. 20:4

EVEN WHILE RISING IN THE early ranks as an airman, one key ingredient to success received from supervisors was "to keep your nose clean." Promotion eligibility was in your hands as long as you met expectations and avoided of trouble.

Folks derived this eighteenth-century English phrase from "keeping one's hands clean," which referred explicitly to avoiding corruption.

God gives success. In 1 Kings 2:3, when King David was about to die, he gave his son, Solomon, the following advice: "Observe what the Lord your God requires: Walk in obedience to him, and keep his decrees and commands, his laws and regulations, as written in the Law of Moses. Do this to prosper in all you do and wherever you go".

In 1 Kings 3:12–14, Solomon's success formula when he became king was to follow God and obey him. He asked the Lord for a discerning heart to govern his people. God answered,

> I will give it to you. I will provide you with a wise and understanding heart. So here is what will be true of you. There has never been anyone like you. And there never will be. And that is not all. So I will give you what you have yet to ask for.
>
> I will give you wealth and honor. As long as you live, no other king will be as great as you are. Live the way I want you to. Obey my laws and commands, just as

your Father David did. Then I will let you live for a long time.

Likewise, you can define your greatest joy or legacy by giving to others and helping someone else grow, prosper, and win. Strive to shift the focus away from yourself.

> *Father, you are my rock, fortress, and deliverer; and I praise you for equipping me for success. I rejoice that I am like a tree firmly planted by the streams of water, ready to bring forth my fruit in my season, and everything I do shall prosper. In your name, I pray, amen.*

Day 3

Promotion

> "I know the plans I have for you," announces the Lord. "I want you to enjoy success. I do not plan to harm you. I will give you hope for the years to come."
> —Jer. 29:11

AS I WAS FLYING IN on a C-17 military transport aircraft to Bagram Airfield, Afghanistan, we began our combat landing approach—a steep dive spiraling down to the airfield below. Soon the pilot's voice came over the intercom: "We have a situation there and must abort our landing and maintain a holding pattern over Bagram at a safe altitude until Airmen can clear the runway."

We circled high above our destination for the next two hours, waiting until authorities cleared us to land.

Life can be like that sometimes. We are eager to reach a destination, be it a unique destination like marriage or a professional goal like earning a college degree or a promotion, but we find that we aren't ready to arrive at a destination, seeing ourselves in what we think is a holding pattern and feeling like we are wasting our time. But the truth is we are still a work in progress, and if we had pushed forward trying to accomplish the right goal at the wrong time, we may have learned some hard lessons we would regret.

When we reflect upon the words of God to the nation of Israel spoken through the prophet Isaiah during a time of exile, we realize that even when things are not going well, he has a plan for us.

Our frustration comes when the fulfillment of a plan seems needlessly slowed down by detours we take in life or other obstacles we run into, but these detours, obstacles, and hardships may even be a piece of his plan for our life.

There is no easy job in today's workplace; every specialty has rigorous training requirements, and you depend upon your coworker to be a subject matter experts at their job. We may want to rush into a supervisory position that we always wanted or get a promotion we think we deserve, but in the end, he may be slowing us down, placing us in a holding pattern because he knows we may not be as ready as we think we are.

But understand this; even holding patterns can help prepare us for what lies ahead, and sometimes we may not know why we have to do everything we do. Still, when our moment arrives, and we finally get to be "the man/woman" or "the boss," we see how much we needed those life lessons and how we may not have been as ready as we thought we were, and that had we pushed forward at the wrong time, things could have ended badly.

Scripture reminds me of how Esther's cousin Mordecai reminded her in Esther 4:14. "You have come to royal position for such a time as this?" Everything Esther had experienced in life up until that point— the good (being selected as the queen of the Medes and Persians), the bad (the death of her parents), and the ugly (the threat of destruction of the Jews)—prepared her for this moment. Esther rose to the challenge by drawing upon her faith and the strength she gained from her experiences. The greatest military, political, or world-changing leaders in our history had to prove themselves in the face of adversity.

> Faith convinces me that there are no wasted experiences in God's great plan. However, we may have brought some bad experiences upon ourselves that he would not have wished us to go through.
>
> But one of the things making him the one true God is that he can take even the worst experiences we have or the most mundane we think there is another holding pattern and weave it into the tapestry of our

life. He prepares us for what opportunities lie ahead in his time.

(Andrew G. McIntosh, former base chaplain at Andersen Air Force Base, Guam)

Father, I bless Your name, El Shaddai, the God Almighty of blessings. You are all-bountiful and all-sufficient. I praise You; in all things, you work for the good of those who love You and have called according to Your purpose. Hallowed be your name! Amen.

Day 4

Diligence

> No matter what you do, work at it with all your might.
> —Eccles. 9:10

WHEN I LIVED AT FORT Myer in Arlington, Virginia, I'd visit Arlington National Cemetery on the weekends and watch the diligence and hard work of the old guard at the Tomb of the Unknown Soldier. Guards are changed every 30 minutes, 24 hours a day, 365 days a year, humbly revering fallen American service members whose remains authorities have not identified. Every sentinel spends five hours a day perfecting their uniform for guard duty and commits two years of life to guard the tomb.

In 2 Thessalonians 3:7–10, Paul also set an excellent example among church members of working hard.

> You know how you should follow our example. We worked when we were with you. We only ate people's food after paying for it. It was just the opposite. We worked night and day. We worked very hard so that we wouldn't cause any expense to any of you. We worked even though we have the right to receive help from you. We did it to be a model for you to follow. Even when we were with you, we gave you a rule. We said, "Anyone who won't work shouldn't be allowed to eat."

The only place success comes before work is in the dictionary. Therefore, your work should never be at such a level where people will liken idleness to God.

The book of Galatians heartens us to let everyone be sure to do his best, for he will have the personal satisfaction of work done well and won't need to compare himself with someone else.

When you strive to be the person God created you to be, you'll find real meaning, purpose, fulfillment, and satisfaction. So stay focused; hard work pays off.

> *Lord, you are an awesome god. Thank you for the grace to continue seeking knowledge and skill in my work areas. My light shall shine before men as they see my good works glorifying you. In Jesus' name, amen.*

Day 5

Balance

> Do your work in six days. But you must rest on the seventh day. So even when plowing your land or gathering your crops, you must rest on the seventh day.
> —Exod. 34:21

ACCORDING TO A FINANCIAL COMPANY survey, roughly three-quarters of Americans live paycheck to paycheck with little to no emergency savings.

I previously worked part-time jobs as a cook, waiter, security guard, and valet parking to pay for bills and other necessities. When your work is out of balance, it can contribute to your spouse's contempt or disrespect because they may feel unloved, insignificant, unvalued, or *second best*.

Psalm 1:1–2 tells us,

> Blessed is the person who obeys the law of the Lord. They don't follow the advice of evil people. Instead, the direction of the Lord gives them joy. They think about his law day and night.

> If we overwork ourselves, we end up spending less time with God. Likewise, Matthew 22:37–38 calls us first to love the Lord, our God with all your heart, soul, and mind because it is the first and greatest commandment.

When overworking causes us to be away from him, we will have lesser time to meditate on His Word!

Matthew 6:24 reminds us that we cannot serve both God and money. Similarly, if you are overworking because you need cash and it is taking you away from him, you must choose between serving him and serving money.

Balance hard work with the other priorities of life. The result of being overworked is more stress coupled with neglected or fractured relationships.

Determine whether the job is too demanding or your work habits need changing. First Corinthians 14:40 tells us to do everything correctly and orderly.

To stay balanced, you first have to help yourself to enable you to help others to the best of your ability.

> *Father, I am so thankful you know my needs. I make my schedule around your Word. With all my heart, I seek You first and your way of doing and being right, and You will take together all my needs and supply me according to your riches in glory. Amen.*

WorkWeek # 3

MODELING ATTRIBUTES OF GODLY EMPLOYEES

Day 1

Prayerfulness

> Daniel found out that the king had signed the order. Despite that, he did just as he had always done before. He went home to his upstairs room. Its windows opened toward Jerusalem. He went to his room three times a day to pray. Finally, he got down on his knees and gave thanks to his God.
> —Dan. 6:10

"IF YOU HAVE EVER THOUGHT about poisoning, choking, punching, or slapping someone you work with, then you need to pray at work."

During my military service, I remember a reference to this "You Need to Pray at Work" email series, which may also apply to your workplace. In addition, many employees also post motivators and scriptures in their workspace to uplift and encourage each other.

You can make work fulfilling, but it can also cause incredible frustration.

Prayer can help put those *dissatisfying* times in perspective. Prayerfulness proved effective from Jesus Christ (Heb. 5:7) to Paul (Col. 1:9) to David (1 Sam. 30:6).

In 1 Chronicles 4:10,

> Jabez cried out to the God of Israel. He said, "I wish you would bless me. Please give me *more* territory. Let your power protect me. Keep me from harm. Then I won't have any pain." God gave him what he asked for.

God wants you to pray about your goals. He wants you to be specific. The more specific you are in your prayers, the quicker he will answer.

He also dares us to ask for extensive requests. James 4:3 says, "When you ask for something, you don't receive it. That's because you ask for the wrong reason." Jeremiah 33:3 tells us, "Call out to me. I will answer you. I will tell you great things you do not know. And unless I do, you wouldn't be able to find out about them." In Matthew 7:7, Jesus said, "Ask, seek, knock" (ASK). Ephesians 3:20 says, "God can do far more than we could ever ask for or imagine. He does everything by his power that is working in us."

Prayer is essential and draws you nearer to God. ASK to make prayer a priority instead of faulting your busy schedule. If you are not praying consistently, your work will suffer. He gives job skills, success, and promotion.

> *Father, this is the confidence I have in you. If I ask anything according to your will, you hear me. I am so thankful that whatever I ask for in prayer, having faith, and believing You will grant it, and I will receive it. You, Father, are honored and glorified. Hallelujah! Amen.*

Day 2

Obedience

> Be careful to obey the terms of this covenant. Then you will have success in everything you do.
> —Deut. 29:9

FROM THE MILITARY, I LEARNED that supervisors expect you to mind your p's and q's and comply with standards of conduct relating not only to the performance of military duties but also to the discharge of your responsibilities, as well as your interactions and relations with other members of the military community.

When I became a federal employee, I underwent a probationary period before my supervisor determined that he had hired the right person and declared me a *regular* employee. You must conform or abide by job standards and expectations at all times, not only during this *trial period*.

In Jesus Christ, we find the perfect model of obedience. He lived a sinless life. He paid for the world's sins and purchased the pardon of men. He also restored man's fellowship with God, opening the way to eternal life.

As his *disciple*, you follow his example as well as his commands. Your motivation for obedience is love. So he tells us in John 14:15, "If you love me, obey my commands."

From the Old to the New Testament, the Bible strongly emphasizes obedience. Therefore, it's good to be involved in worship at church. Please continue to praise him through your daily obedience as you move out into the real world. In your job, obedience brings blessings.

Father, in the name of Jesus, I commit myself to walk in the Word. In your name and obedience to your will, I yield my desires not in your plan. Amen.

Day 3

Attitude

> Finally, my brothers and sisters always think about what is true. Think about what is noble, right, and pure. Think about what is lovely and worthy of respect. If anything is excellent or worthy of praise, think about those kinds of things.
>
> —Phil. 4:8

ACCORDING TO A RECENT GALLUP survey, 90 percent of the employees surveyed said they were at least satisfied with their jobs. Building and maintaining healthy, effective relationships in all directions with people you work with and people who work for you is one of the keys to job satisfaction. People who excel always maintain a positive attitude.

I strive to start my day with God first, shaping the Spirit of my mind to give my best and staying in faith throughout the day.

In Philippians 1:27, Paul also writes from a prison cell in Rome about the attitude a Christian should have: "No matter what happens, live in a way that brings honor to the good news about Christ." He's telling us that no matter what unexpected disruptions, frustrations, or difficulties come our way, we respond with Christlike attitudes.

Paul later writes in Philippians 2:5, "As you deal with one another, you should think and act as Jesus did." He also encourages us in Ephesians 5:1 and Matthew 5:16, respectively, to "*follow his [God's] example*" and "in the same way, let your light shine so others can see it. Then they will see the good things you do. And they will bring glory to your Father who is in heaven."

At or outside work, strive to embody a Christlike attitude—selflessness, humility, and service. Regardless of how big or small the job is, give it your best. Great performers give their best effort no matter the size of the audience.

Your attitude determines your joy. Proverbs 12:24 tell us, Hands that work hard will rule. But lazy people will be forced to work.

Father, whatever is true, worthy of reverence, honorable, pure, lovely and lovable, kind, winsome, and gracious; if there is any virtue and excellence or worthy of praise, I will think on and weigh and fix my mind on them. Amen.

Day 4

Encouragement

> So encourage one another with the hope you have.
> Build each other up. That's what you are doing.
> —1 Thess. 5:11

ONE OF MY RESPONSIBILITIES AS a base communications security manager was to perform a combination change on a security container when needed.

One time during this procedure, I missed a validation step. As a result, I locked out everyone from the safe container—both unauthorized and authorized users. I kept a secure environment!

Combination troubleshooting to open the high-security electromechanical lock was unsuccessful. But I felt miserable about the situation; it wasn't one of my better moments.

When a female coworker reported for duty from unit physical training, she saw my distress. After explaining the setback, she confided, "The world isn't over. We'll get the container open." I kept my chin up, and her positive words encouraged me; contractors drilled the lock and replaced it with a spare.

In John 16:33, Jesus also encouraged his followers, "In this world, you will have trouble. But be encouraged! I have won the battle over the world." He did not shy away from telling his followers about the troubles they would face. He told them the world would hate them (John 15:18–21). But his grim forecast was tempered with cheer.

He followed his prediction of trouble with a sparkling word of encouragement: He has overcome the world. Jesus is more significant than any trouble we face.

Scripture tells us to encourage one another. Similarly, when providing performance feedback, you help ensure your employees know where they stand and how to improve.

You can set people up for success or failure by your expectations. Treat them as they could be to bring out the best in those around you. Tell it like it could be.

> *Father, you are great and greatly to be praised. I am the righteousness of you. I purpose to edify my neighbor, encourage, strengthen, and build up others according to their needs. Amen.*

Day 5

Faithfulness

> A faithful person will be richly blessed. But anyone who wants to get rich will be punished.
> —Prov. 28:20

WHEN I LIVED IN GUAM, our men's ministry headed a bimonthly homeless feeding, monthly breakfast, prison fellowship ministry, family fun day, and retreat, among other outreach activities. I'm so grateful I was part of a group exemplifying "as iron sharpens iron" and striving to be "complete in Christ."

Actions speak louder than words, and being in the men's ministry was a powerful way of spreading the good news by demonstrating it daily. A faith lived is a robust and attractive faith.

Scripture speaks often of God's faithfulness. When he says he will do something, he does it. With Him, all things are possible (Matt. 19:26). He is the same yesterday, today, and forever. If this were not the case if he were unfaithful even *once*, he would not be God, and we would be unable to rely of his promises. But as it is, "Every single word of those promises has come true." (1 Kings 8:56).

God is faithful. Faithfulness is an essential part of who he is (Ps. 89:8, Heb. 13:8).

The heroic men and women of the "hall of faith" or the "faith hall of fame" in Hebrews 11 encourage and challenge you to grow your faith.

In Daniel 6:4, he influenced his employer, one of the most influential people in the world, to believe in the only true God. By doing a job well in your sphere of work, you can also practically "show and tell" others with whom you work about Christ.

Father, in the name of Jesus, I cast my care on you. I expect a life of victory because I do my actions on behalf of a spirit humbly submitted to your truth and righteousness. So may your will be done on earth in my life as it is in heaven. Amen.

WorkWeek # 4

LEADING AND BEYOND

Day 1

Direction

Trust in the Lord with all your heart. Refrain from depending on your understanding. Instead, in all your ways, obey him. Then he will make your paths smooth and straight.

—Prov. 3:5–6

"WHAT WILL I DO WHEN I finish high school?" is a question many students ask. For some, the answer is "get a job." For others, the answer is "to travel and see the world or to continue education." I decided to "continue my education" at a local college before enlisting in the United States Air Force to "see the world." The immediate result of my decision was gratefully serving my country.

However, I obligingly experienced many second and third-order consequences, which were different yet directly linked to my initial decision—the permanent change of station or assignment; unaccompanied tours; temporary duty including short- or no-notice deployments, alerts, recalls, extended hours, or shift work; and the real possibility of making the ultimate sacrifice in the line of duty.

In Jeremiah 42:8–22, the people of Judah also stood at a crossroads and on the cusp of a significant decision. God inflicted their nation with disaster. They believed Egypt to the south offered more stability and protection from the dreaded Babylonian armed forces.

The people asked Jeremiah, a prophet, for God's advice. After ten days of waiting, Jeremiah returned with an answer. He promised them two things: "If you stay here in the land I have given you, I will restore your land. But if you go to Egypt, you will all depart this life." Their desired outcome propelled them to "pitch their tent" in Egypt; they made a choice based on their wisdom and direction versus his, and they eventually passed away.

If you display your faith in obedience to God, the decision of confidence in your life will always lead you down the right path. He is with you. I know the plans I have for you, announces the Lord. I want you to enjoy success. I do not plan to harm you. On the contrary, I will give you hope for the years to come (Jer. 29:11).

> *Father, in Jesus's name, I praise you. I thank you for ordering my steps and instructing me in the way which I should go. Thank you for your guidance and leadership concerning your will, plan, and purpose for my life. As I follow you, Lord, my daily path becomes more evident. Amen.*

Day 2

Communication

> All these people are united and speak the same language. That is why they can do all this. Now they will be able to do anything they plan.
> —Gen. 11:6

YOU MAY BE FAMILIAR WITH the test man or the Verizon guy character in Verizon Wireless's "Can you hear me now?" commercials. You may also feel frustrated when you feel like you're not being listened to, others change the subject, thus invalidating your feelings, and when others behave in a way showing inattention.

When communicating with my spouse, we don't always get it right, but we always strive to give each other our undivided attention. Listening to each person's words is essential to show value and respond appropriately.

The Genesis account of building the Tower of Babel also supports the importance of good communication. Everyone spoke the same language and adopted a common goal. The Lord makes this remarkable observation stated above in Genesis 11:6.

When people have good communication and pursue a common goal, "nothing they plan to do will be impossible for them" as long as it is within the will of God.

Since building the tower was different from what he wanted, construction stopped. In addition, he disrupted their ability to communicate, which was the foundation for the successful completion of the tower.

> "Come on! Let us go down and mix up their language. Then they will not be able to understand one other."
> (Gen. 11:7).

It is vital to listen to employee complaints.

> Suppose I haven't treated any of my male and female servants fairly when they've brought charges against me. Then what will I do when God opposes me? What answer will I give him when he asks me to explain myself?
>
> (Job 31:13–14)

A sensitive listening ear is a tangible expression of care. When an employee presents a problem and solution, employers should take appropriate steps to solve the problem.

> *Father, I desire to be in accord with James 1:19 and be quick to listen, slow to speak, and slow to become angry. I purpose to express truth in all things and be filled with your praise and honor all day. In Jesus's name, amen.*

Day 3

Ambition

Don't do anything only to get ahead. Please don't do it because you are proud. Instead, be humble. Value others more than yourselves.

—Phil. 2:3

WHEN I BECAME A HIGH-LEVEL manager, I had the opportunity to conduct airmen calls or meetings. Unfortunately, the junior enlisted frequently perceived the senior noncommissioned officers as all about *me*. Instead of caring for their people and fulfilling duty expectations, subordinates sensed the senior leader advancing on personal interests by showing, "I want to get promoted." "Number one," "the best," and "bigger and better" is analogous to ambition. Your desire for promotion and initiative is in line; what one esteems, or honors needs to be revised.

In Galatians 1:10, Paul also addressed ambition by posing an insightful question: "Am I now trying to get people to think well of me? Or do I want God to think well of me? Am I trying to please people? If I were, I would not be serving Christ." So is your ambition to please him or to please man?

In seeking and honoring him, he assures you of his profound promise: "But put God's kingdom first. Do what he wants you to do. Then all those things will also be given to you." (Matt. 6:33).

Scripture supports ambition. To please Christ, work hard, and pursue excellence in your job. Your motive is suitable when your success helps others rather than others mistaking it as a selfish act.

When your peers are promoted right over your head, and the promotion system *passes you over*, celebrate and commend their success. Be grateful, not regretful. Scripture says It is better to be satisfied with what you have than always to want something else. So rejoice in what you have. Your time is coming, not now. Continue to do your work well.

> *Father, you are the great "I Am." I appreciate your grace to shine upon me. I seek your kingdom and ask you to help me see my situation as you see it and as you want it to be. I claim your blessings and thank you for the favor, increase, and overflow at my place of employment, at home, or wherever I may be. In Jesus's name, amen.*

Day 4

Team

Commit to the Lord in everything you do. Then he will make your plans succeed.
—Prov. 16:3

A friend of mine shared this testimony:

As a military spouse for over 29 years, I accompanied my husband worldwide, working for several employers. I am an educator and worked in seven different school districts and nine schools. The Lord blessed me with a job for each of our military relocations. God is good: employers hired me, and I also started teaching the first year school year after our transfer to each new base.

Looking back at each school I've taught in, I see the reason the Lord placed me at each school. Whether it was helping a child who adults abused, befriending a lonely colleague far from home, supporting a child with a learning disability, or mentoring a young teacher and mother, I am thankful for the opportunities I have had to serve the Lord through my chosen field.
(Tonya Byrd)

PROVERBS 31 SPEAKS OF "A wife of noble character." She worked hard to keep her house and her family in order.

In providing for her family, her employment was secondary to the stewardship of her husband, children, and home. (Gen. 2:18, Prov. 31:10–31). However, no Bible verse prohibits a woman from working outside the home. Women maintained jobs outside their homes, from Deborah, Anna, Tabitha, and Phoebe to Rahab.

Many couples and families struggle to embrace this biblical "Proverbs 31" model of a spouse working outside the home.

When you commit yourselves to build a successful lifelong marriage, you act as wise captains and recognize, lean on, and use each other's strengths to benefit the entire family. "Two people are better than one. They can help each other in everything they do. Suppose either of them falls. Then one can help the other one up." (Eccles. 4:9–10).

> *Father, we decree and declare ourselves to agree to live in mutual harmony and accord. We thank you that our marriage grows stronger daily in the bond of unity because it is founded on your Word and rooted and grounded in your love. In the mighty name of Jesus, amen.*

Day 5

Transitioning

> But my life means nothing to me. My only goal is to finish the race. I want to complete the work the Lord Jesus has given me. He wants me to tell others about the good news of God's grace.
>
> —Acts 20:24

THE DICTIONARY DEFINES *RETIREMENT*: "withdrawal from an occupation, a retreat from active life." Your culture may promote the goal of retirement as ceasing all labor to live a life filled with leisure.

In 2011, serving as the Guam retiree activities office director, I wrote an article titled "The Bottom LINE How Retirees, Active-duty Stay Connected."

Retirement is becoming a time of high activity and purpose instead of unproductiveness. According to the Association of American Retired Persons (AARP), 45 percent of all pre-retirees expect to continue working into their seventies or later—nearly half of all Americans aged fifty-five and over volunteer.

You may be out of the service, but work hasn't served you out. You are still operating in heart and Spirit. You may have retired, but you are in no way tired. Growing older, you still use your talents and skills to help others. Like academic graduation, retirement is when you move on to new, bigger, and better things.

Bible verses about retirement encourage you to put God first to help make wise decisions. For example, in Numbers 8:24–26, God informed Moses that the Levite priests working in the Tabernacle must retire. In the passage, God tells us that "they must retire from their regular service and work no longer" and "they [the retired

Levites] may assist their brothers in performing their duties, but they must not do the work."

While physically and mentally capable, don't let age stop you from finishing God's work. He will provide you with the necessary strength. For example, Moses was eighty years old when he began a forty-year journey leading the children of Israel.

Instead of being put "out to pasture," shift gears and use your experience and wisdom to open doors to new and different ways of serving God and others. Every exit is an entry. *Retirement* is not the end; it's the beginning of your next chapter in life. Help others during your retirement years.

> *Father, I bless your name, Jehovah-Jireh, who sees my needs and provides for them. I commit this transition to you, knowing you shall direct my path. I praise you. I am strong and doing what is right, letting not my hands be weak or slack or my heart weary of serving you. Amen.*

Acknowledgments

DREAMS AND TEAMS WORK TOGETHER, and many people assisted me in preparing this text. I love when a plan comes together.

But, first and foremost, I thank Almighty God! He enabled me with faithfulness, gifts, and favor. The pen is mightier than the sword, and may all I put my hands to bring glory to his kingdom.

While reviewing this devotional in manuscript form, I'm also grateful for the synergy of wise counsel and inspiring insights and expertise from ministers and pastors. Thank you, team!

Additionally, I appreciate those who prayed and supported me in writing this book. I hope that these multiplied blessings touch your heart. Lord God Almighty, make your face shine upon me. Make it possible for the most significant number of new and growing believers to draw nearer to you!

Appendixes

Appendix A

Additional Topic Bible Verses

Workweek # 1
Day 1 Prov. 10:9, 11:3, 12:22, 19:1, 28:6
Day 2 Gal. 5:13, James 2:18; Matt. 20:26–28, 1 Pet. 4:9–11
Day 3 Dan. 5:12, 6:3; Phil. 1:9–10, 4:8
Day 4 1 Chron. 17:25–26, 2 Chron. 32:7–8, Deut. 31:6, Heb. 3:6, John 16:33, Josh. 1:6–9, Phil. 1:19–21
Day 5 1 Cor. 16:13–14; Prov. 17:17, 18:24; Matt. 26:33

Workweek # 2
Day 1 Col. 3:23–24; Eccles. 10:10; Eph. 2:10, 3:20; Exod. 20:9; Gen. 1:12; Isa. 54:2; 2 Pet. 1:10; Phil. 3:13; 2 Thess. 3:10–12
Day 2 Gen. 39:2–3; James 4:10; 1 Kings 2:3; Matt. 16:26; Phil. 4:13; Prov. 3:1–4, 16:3, 22:29; Ps. 1:1–6, 37:4
Day 3 Col. 3:23; Dan. 2:48; Gen. 12:2; James 4:10; Ps. 1:1–3, 20:4, 75:6–7; Rom. 8:28; 2 Tim. 2:15
Day 4 2 Pet. 1:10; Prov. 12:24, 12:27, 21:5, 22:29; Ps. 119:4
Day 5 Prov. 6:6–11, 12:27, 18:9; 2 Thess. 3:7–9

Workweek # 3
Day 1 James 1:5; Prov. 4:7, 9:9, 16:16; Ps. 104:5
Day 2 Deut. 11:26–28; Eph. 2:10; James 1:25; Job 36:11; John 14:15; Luke 11:28; Phil. 4:13; Ps. 119:44, 60, 101

Day 3 Acts 17:11; 1 Cor. 2:16; 2 Cor. 10:5; Ephes. 4:23; Isa. 26:3; Matt. 26:41; 1 Pet. 1:13; Phil. 4:8; Rom. 7:25, 12:2
Day 4 Josh. 1:9; Prov. 30:5; Ps. 121:1–8, 37:4; 2 Tim. 1:749
Day 5 1 Cor. 4:2, Luke 16:12, Matt. 25:21, Prov. 28:20, Ps. 31:23, 1 Tim. 1:12

Workweek # 4
Day 1 Gal. 5:16; James 1:5; Prov. 3:5–6, 11:3, 16:3; Ps. 37:23, 121:8, 138:8
Day 2 Gen. 1:1–31, James 1:1–27, Prov. 10:11
Day 3 Luke 2:52; Prov. 3:3–4; Ps. 5:12, 84:11
Day 4 Col. 3:18–19; 1 Cor. 7:3; Deut. 6:6–9; Eph. 5:22, 5:25; Gen. 2:24; Heb. 13:4; Prov. 5:18–19, 12:4, 14:1, 18:22, 19:14, 31:31
Day 5 James 4:1–2; 1 John 2:16; John 5:44; Matt. 4:8–10, 6:33, 23:5–7, 23:12; Rom. 12:16; 1 Tim. 6:9

Appendix B

One Body but Many Parts (1 Cor. 12:12–31)

JUST AS A BODY, THOUGH one has many parts, all its features form one body, so it is with Christ. We were all baptized by one Spirit to form one body—whether Jews or Gentiles, enslaved person or free—and we were all given the one Spirit to drink. But, even so, the body comprises not one part but many.

Now if the foot should say, "Because I am not a hand, I do not belong to the body," it would not, for that reason, stop being part of the body. And if the ear should say, "Because I am not an eye, I do not belong to the body," it would not, for that reason, stop being part of the body. Where *would* the sense of hearing be if the whole body *were* an eye? Where *would* the sense of smell be if the entire body were an ear? But in fact, God has placed the parts in the body, every one of them, just as he wanted them to be. If they were all one part, where *would* the body *be*? As it is, *there are* many parts, but one body.

The eye cannot say to the hand, "I don't need you!" And the head cannot say to the feet, "I don't need you!" On the contrary, those parts of the body that folks see as weaker are indispensable, and we treat the *details* that we think are less honorable with special honor. And the unpresentable features are treated with special modesty, while our presentable parts need no special treatment. But God has put the body together, giving more incredible honor to the *factors* that lacked it so that there should be no division in the body but *that* its parts should have equal concern for each other.

If one part suffers, every part suffers; if one part is honored, every part rejoices.

Now you are the body of Christ, and each of you is a part of it. And God has placed in the church first of all apostles, second prophets, third teachers, then miracles, then gifts of healing, helping, guiding, and different kinds of tongues. *Are* all apostles? *Are* all prophets? *Are* all teachers? *Do* all work miracles? Do all have gifts of healing? Do all speak with tongues? Do all interpret? Now eagerly desire more significant contributions.

Finally, Review Ask

You love this book. Remember to leave a review! I welcome your feedback to help improve your reader experience.

I'd also be grateful if you'd leave an honest review for me on Amazon, Goodreads, BookBub, or markcoverton.com.

Help share God's Word and let me know the truth about *Crossroads*! Your support in the form of a review does make a difference. I read all the reviews and use your feedback to help pen books for you even better.

https://www.amazon.com/author/markoverton
https://www.goodreads.com/author/show/7647613.Mark_C_Overton
https://www.bookbub.com/profile/mark-c-overton

You can also request an Authorgraph at: https://www.authorgraph.com/authors/goodnewsbookset.

Draw nearer to God and draw God nearer to you, and "Like" our page at: https://www.facebook.com/YourWordIsTruthAlways/ to help the masses.

I thank you endlessly. Every review makes a difference, and it matters a *lot!*

ALSO, READ OTHER BOOKS BY MARK C. OVERTON

"True Words for True Believers"

LORD, Teach Me How to Pray, 2nd edition.

Faith Series
Faith Excellence
Faith Transformation

The Good Book Series
New Day, New Life (Series Compilation)
What Love Really Means
You Only Live Once
I Like to Start with Something Funny
LORD, Teach Me How to Pray
Chapter and Verse
Airmen Series
Career Progression Guide for Airmen: The Basics
Career Progression Guide for Airmen

BONUS BOOK CONTENT

I can only offer so much within this book; however, this book is just the start, and you can view trailers for each book at: https://youtube.com/@truewordsalways

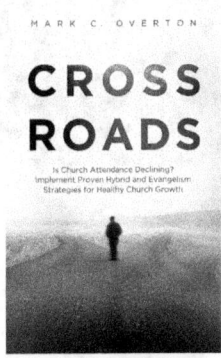

ABOUT THE AUTHOR

MARK C. OVERTON is a retired Chief Master Sergeant, the highest enlisted rank in the U.S. Air and Space Force. As a lifelong follower of Jesus, he continued his next assignment of spreading the Gospel, inspiring him to create and share Christian Life Devotionals. Mark writes with a heart of compassion and service to serve his readers and instantly change lives. His message aims to refresh, encourage, empower your perspective, and draw you nearer to God.

Mark actively attends and teams with the First Assembly of God in North Little Rock, Arkansas. In addition, he completed the Dallas Theological Seminary's Master of Biblical and Theological degree program in 2020. Mark also partnered with Joel Osteen Ministries as a "Champion of Hope" and participated in an interview with Dr. Angela Butts Chester, "Daily Spark Radio and T.V." host.

www.ingramcontent.com/pod-product-compliance
Lightning Source LLC
LaVergne TN
LVHW011739060526
838200LV00051B/3258